Walking Trees
and Other Poems

poems by

Steven Peterson

With a Foreword by Jill Peláez Baumgaertner

Finishing Line Press
Georgetown, Kentucky

Walking Trees
and Other Poems

Publisher: Leah Huete de Maines
Editor: Christen Kincaid
Cover Art: Steven Peterson
Author Photo: Chris Popio, Popio Stumpf Photography, Chicago.
Cover Design: Elizabeth Maines McCleavy

Order online: www.finishinglinepress.com
also available on amazon.com

Author inquiries and mail orders:
Finishing Line Press
PO Box 1626
Georgetown, Kentucky 40324
USA

Contents

Foreword by Jill Peláez Baumgaertner

IV. Readings

V. Northwoods

for Betsy

Foreword

Read this book of poems cover to cover, and you will know the bounty that is Steven Peterson. There is so much to know—from the difficult birth of a child with a failing heart, to life during the pandemic, to an account of the poet's first hunt when he, as a child, disastrously shot a small squirrel instead of the grouse he thought it was. You will find surprises on every page, and poems that do what poems should do—upset the usual. What emerges is a three-dimensional picture created from the glimpses he affords you, much like the scene he describes as he walks a Dutch street, appreciating the peeks he observes of evening life in a culture that does not draw its curtains shut.

Peterson retired early from an international career as a business writer so that he could focus on playwriting, which was remarkably successful until the pandemic which closed the theatres. He had already begun to write poems, and so shortly before the pandemic, he submitted one of the strongest Advent poems that I, as poetry editor of *The Christian Century*, had read. After two more acceptances, Steve and I met for coffee and a rousing and encouraging conversation about poetry and faith, which some consider an anathematic combination. But it is faith that undergirds these poems—faith in the face of the terrible loss of a child at age eight. This is faith which creates sudden insights as he remembers his past—for example, how his 5th grade teacher responded to him impetuously calling her by her first name. This is faith which catches him reading as he sits lakeside while a storm approaches.

> And yet I find I can't read long,
>
> because I'd rather read the sky
> whose author writes, *Just take your time*
> *and watch. Now talk to me. I'm here.*

But Steve also writes with biting insights as in one my favorites, "Falling," which always elicits, with its pointed last line, a kind of knowing laughter. Peterson does this well as he writes about the Apocalypse or gives a "When Harry met Sally" version of Christ and the woman at the well or describes a "Zoom Bible Study," which contains the familiar claims of Christ ("I am the Alpha and the Omega") ironically interspersed with all of the frustrating Zoom clichés that populate every group meeting ("You're on mute.").

Peterson's best poems, however, happen when he combines his personal experience within the larger story, the rhythms of the church calendar, the stories from Scripture that form the Great Code, as Northrop Frye calls it. In "Advent," which is the final poem in the book, he lulls us into the comfort and coziness of a drink by the fire and early bedtime in a deserted northern town. Stepping outside for more wood, however, he senses "a constant trembling." This is Advent. "Someone surely there, someone almost here."

Peterson knows of the grand reality behind our everydayness, of Eliot's fragments shored up against our ruin. These poems—about theatre, about children, about world travels and church services, about Longfellow, Elvis, and Willa Cather, about stories from Scripture, are filled with humor and pathos and the deepest, dearest understanding of what it means to be human, anchored in the earth while reaching for the transcendent, sometimes just out of reach, sometimes almost touching its delicate webs.

Jill Peláez Baumgaertner
Chicago, 2024

I. Cities

The Sorrows of Migration

They navigate by stars at night,
The moon, and some magnetic field,
North up the Mississippi Flyway
In spring, or south in fall, concealed
By darkness from our human sight.

Migrating birds by millions pass
Through overhead while we're asleep,
But in Chicago, birds that die may
Be found each dawn in feathered heaps—
Killed by striking our walls of glass.

Skyscraper lights attract them in,
Their navigation gets thrown off,
And creatures used to field and forest
Collide a thousand feet aloft
With what to them has never been.

We gather bodies one by one
In every color of creation,
Our songbirds now a silent chorus.
We grieve the sorrows of migration,
Still building till we reach the sun.

The Glorious Order of Things

When Bradford came, our friend's autistic boy,
We put him in our guest room with his mom.
He doesn't talk. He watches. That's his joy.
Sometimes he gets upset; most times he's calm.
The second day he wandered off alone,
Climbing the stairs to where I keep my den.
We heard him there—a floorboard creak, a moan.
His mother said he's fine; we talked again.

That night I saw what Bradford did: My books
Had all been taken down from shelves and piled
In patterns, somehow based upon their looks.
I stood awhile deciphering, then smiled
At perfect order—color, shape, and size—
For he saw things through brighter, gloried eyes.

This Week's Deaths by Guns in Chicago

1.

They point a gun, they ask him for his shoes,
he gives his shoes, but still they shoot him dead,
and he'll be buried deep in the day's news
in cap and gown—*Nice smile*, the man had said.

The day that photo clicked, he now recalls
while lying in his blood, he looked ahead
to something growing dim, hearing footfalls
echoing down the alley till he's dead.

Not quite. He thinks, *What's next?* He hears the cries
at church. He wishes he can sing along
(although he can't, no matter how he tries)
to "Precious Lord," his mother's favorite song.

He knows he'll look at peace, and with that smile
inside, happy he was loved for a while.

2.

On Sunday morning, up on the North Side,
his name appears among the listed ones
our own fine church now reads of those who died,
typeset neatly in "This Week's Deaths by Guns."

Bowing our heads, we parents peek around
to see if others do what we will do:
repeat each name in whispers, holding sound
until those many names are prayed on through.

But you, O Lord, can sense our prayer inside:
*May murders stay confined to neighborhoods
to which we rarely go.* We try to hide
our secret, shameful thought; we know we should,

because each name, each name, when all is done,
is our own precious daughter, precious son.

Beautiful Are the Feet

The actors stand and strut and dance and fight
all barefoot in the sand, for here tonight
a play director noted in our age
has mounted *Romeo and Juliet*
within a giant sandbox on the stage.

I'm watching this familiar play, endearing,
immortal, tragic, yet deep down I'm hearing
beautiful are the feet of messengers
who bring good news—Isaiah, isn't it?—
seeing what of us is shared and, yes, endures:

the ankle bone, the arching underfoot,
the balanced way the toes splay out when put
down in the sand. And though they're many raced
and gendered, all the actors play as one,
stage lit and splendored, like a lush foretaste.

For in the rush of scenes and rowdy crowds
they stir up atmospheres of knee-high clouds,
settling as sand dust on their common feet,
faint messages of what we hope will come
when playing's done, in paradise we meet.

Going Through a Church Split

Cathedral elms once graced our street
   Before they cut them down.
As rot seeped into greenery,
   On came a chain-saw sound.

Cathedral elms were God's sure sign
   Our way of life was true,
Their Gothic-arching branches seemed
   To point us straight to You.

We lived our lives in sweet green shade,
   All summer we stayed cool.
Our trees constrained the fiery sun
   From scorching every fool.

Our trees are gone. The sun beats down.
   There is no summer shade.
Our church split—now we fools can see
   The desert we have made.

Storefront Theater

Chicago. January. Prior time.
"The core of winter," says our weatherman,
Whose forecast draws more eyes than local crime
Or something happening in Somewheristan.
A storefront theater. A wind-chilled night.
We're in a tiny lobby, parka-packed.
A call: "The house is open now!" Polite,
We set out folding chairs from where they're stacked.
Lights down. Lights up. Two actors: He and She.
Her voice. Then his. They whisper; we're that near.
Who now recalls the winter? Nobody.
We're anywhere. It's anytime. For here,
Between that simple stage and every seat,
A kind of cold communion turns to heat.

Ghost Light

We closed our theaters—a silence rules.
Homebound with Internet and iPhones, stocked

with everything we'd want as hoarding fools,
we double check to see our doors are locked.

Elizabethans closed their theaters
in plague years; Shakespeare scribbled poems for praises.

Today each playwright (one is me) utters
in keyboard clacks: free verse or formal phrases.

Yet theaters keep one bare light bulb burning
on stage, illuminating emptiness.

Tradition calls it a "ghost light," discerning
substance from shadows—like our faithfulness.

Let's ask the ghost light of our soul: Explain
this wait for life, or death, or deathless gain.

Church Going Online

Altar bare.
No one's there.
It's unused.

Where the Word
once was heard:
empty pews.

It lies dark
and was marked
unessential.

Can a screen
ever seem
reverential?

Fearful Prayer of a High-Rise Developer

Luke 16:19-24

Dear Lord, my latest high-rise plan is this:
fabulous views, a Starbucks down the block,
security with cameras you can't miss,
and rooftop tracks where dogs can take a walk.
I'm filling up my neighborhood with these
apartment towers built for city life
(just keep us separate from the homeless, please,
who beg along our street, upset my wife,
and interrupt a pleasant shopping trip).
Some nights I fear the flames where I'll be flung.
That beggar—will he dip a fingertip
in water so it cools my burning tongue?
It's night. I look down at the street and see
my beggar looking up and straight at me.

Our Neighbor Who Now Waits

I wait, each day these days like all the rest.
I wake, I dress, I walk the dog at eight.
I breakfast, feed the dog, clean up the mess,
then watch the television while I wait.

At noon it's time to walk the dog again.
I talk, if talk at all, to mutter "hi's"
to nameless women and to nameless men
whose dogs, oddly, have names I recognize.

After a lunch for me with scraps for dog,
I organize our photo albums till
sleepiness saturates the room like fog.
I nap. The dog curled by me also will.

There's gloom when I wake up. The dog still sleeps.
The room seems strange. I dreamt of you; it was
that dream you had returned. The dog wakes, leaps
off of the bed and to the door because

at four we always take another walk.
We fetch the mail: junk mail, a catalog,
another bill. Then dinnertime. I talk,
if talk at all, to reassure the dog

that you'll return to us in just a few more days.
The dog can't comprehend but dips its snout
back in the bowl as if my words were praise,
for that's what dogs want: praise and going out.

At eight I walk the dog for one last time,
thinking about what humans want: like what
dogs want but more? Yet in my pantomime
of signs there is no way to tell the mutt

that you are never coming back; you can't.
Dogs just don't understand that, nor do I.
I'd rather watch dogs wag their tails and pant,
happy and hopeful, trust bright in their eyes.

Elegy for Eulogies

Sometimes we were surprised
or not
but always we felt bad
to hear
there'll be no funeral
no kind
of memorial service
no way
to celebrate those lives
beyond
a pixeled program on
a screen.

All of us did our best
but still
it seemed like standing at
the graves
of souls forever marked
Unknown.

Bowl of Strawberries, Bowl of Milk

It probably wasn't my best idea,
during the worst of Covid,
to stream Ingmar Bergman's
1957 film *The Seventh Seal*
set during the 1350 bubonic plague,
because nearly every character dies—
in black and white and in Swedish.

But then I reached the scene
where the grim medieval knight
encounters a poor traveling family—
mother, father, and infant—
who shares with him their simple supper:
a bowl of strawberries
and a bowl of milk.

The knight takes what he is offered,
then says, according to the subtitles:
I shall remember this moment,
your faces in the evening light,
and carry this memory between my hands
as carefully as if it were a bowl
filled to the brim with fresh milk.
It will be a sign; it will be enough for me.

II. Overseas

Foreign Studies

Twenty-six jet-lagged college kids
arrive in Freiburg, Germany,
starting their semester abroad.
On their first day they tour the *Altstadt*
under a low, cold, winter sun.
Around a great Gothic cathedral
is a wide cobbled *Münsterplatz*
where they try out their classroom German—
Ich möchte Mittagessen kaufen—
for bratwurst from a food-truck grill.

Revived by lunch and winter's chill,
they enter the cathedral, finding
its stony darkness colder still.
For here their guide, a local woman,
once a girl who had witnessed it,
tells them about the War—*der Krieg*—
when nearly every Freiburg building
was burned one night by Allied planes.
She says those planes spared this cathedral;
the bombers used its cross—*"ihr Kreuz,*
what God could see if looking down"—
as a reference point to drop their loads
around a cross soon ringed with fire.
Four years before this, she then adds,
all of the Jews in town were seized
and later murdered in the camps.

She looks at them with such deep sorrow
none of them knows quite what to say.
What these students may say, someday,
is what they now begin to learn.

Singapore Men's Bible Study

We take our shoes off, leave them by the door,
And sit in batik shirts and khaki shorts
In Paul's colonial house in Singapore.

These bungalows, called "black and whites"—the sorts
In travel ads: black timbered, whitewashed walled—
Raise ghosts of Empire dealing imports/exports.

Tonight, we expat businessmen sit sprawled
In wicker chairs along Paul's wicker bar
Because a Bible verse left us appalled.

It's this: "Tomorrow you will travel far
To buy and sell and count your business gains,
But soon you'll vanish like a falling star."

Outside Paul's house the pelting tropic rains
Return to bring the heavy jungle scent
Of flowers rotting down to their remains,

Repeating, with our beers, what that verse meant.

Matisse After the Liberation

I didn't want to tell. He was my father
And I his only daughter, Marguerite.
Just after my escape I wrote him letters
Describing tortures I received as "hard
Interrogation," sparing him the truth.
France was being liberated. Why say more?

It took three months that fall for me to heal,
If one can ever heal. I never cried.
My father taught me to endure. I did.
That final winter of the war I traveled
South to his house and studio near Nice.
I owed him that—to show him I survived.

He wasn't well. He painted in a wheelchair.
Each afternoon we talked into the dusk.
Finally, I told him all the Nazis did.
At first, he didn't speak. As usual,
He spoke in paint—his colors now looked bruised
And soon he stopped his painting altogether.

He turned to paper cutouts he had fashioned
When I was young. His colors breathed again.
He turned, surprisingly, to that new chapel
Designed with his own Stations of the Cross
Where people worshipped as he never could.
I may be wrong. His art was his own way.

Apocalypse Is Beautiful

Apocalypse is beautiful
when seen from far away.
Our latest telescope retells
a distant disarray:

Two galaxies collide, one dies,
and yet we do not weep,
but say, "What colors! What design!"
and get a good night's sleep.

Dutch Windows

Walking through Hoofddorp in the autumn dusk
I pass a row of houses, brick and square,
each with a large plate-glass window exposing
a neat and tidy living room inside.
I heard somewhere the Dutch don't draw their shades,
don't close their curtains, even at night.
They need to show they have nothing to hide.

Is this some remnant of their once-held faith?
Whatever the reason for their odd habit,
they've clearly kept it up, so now I view
a mother at her laptop by a lamp,
a child practicing a mute piano,
a father in a track suit passing through,
all in a picture frame, a stage-like cube.

Dutch windows and Dutch art mix in my mind
while those I watch slip back four centuries,
dress for its age, and pose as in the past,
completely still, yet animated by
pure gesture and expression, linking life
to light from one clear source, making us look,
and look, until that light is gone at last.

At the Comédie-Française

How does one tell the sad from funny stuff
In these obsessive characters on stage?
Alas, my French was never good enough.

One character seems ill. Is it a bluff?
Another hates us all. Just jealous rage?
How does one tell the sad from funny stuff?

I speak some French but it is pretty rough
(Although I understand more on a page).
Alas, my French was never good enough.

When actors speak Molière it's much too tough
For me to follow and I disengage.
How does one tell the sad from funny stuff?

My comprehension isn't up to snuff
So I'm trapped, monolingual, in a cage.
Alas, my French was never good enough.

These comedies are tragedies that puff
Away pretentions I'm a cultured sage.
How does one tell the sad from funny stuff?
Alas, my French was never good enough.

Twapandula

The Central Highlands of Angola go
dry in their wintertime, May to October,
when those of us on building projects fly
America to Cape Town to Luanda
and then by prop plane to a countryside
of refugees returning to their land.

There are no animals. There are no birds.
The fields are full of warning signs, ignored.
To pick their corn they send their children out
because they're lighter, less likely to trip
a land mine left from a long civil war.
In villages we visit, building schools
where schools had been erased, we see some kids
who lost a leg or two, in wheelchairs made
from disconnected bicycle wheels strapped
to legless chairs from their colonial past.

At night, when finished with our cornmeal dinner,
we sit around a bonfire after dark
as the Angolans teach us songs of praise.
One song we learn is titled "Twapandula."
It's the Umbundu language word for thank you.
The lyrics repeat *Twapandula, thank you.*
The sparks from our fire rise to a sky
clearer and deeper than we've ever seen.
We all sing *Twapandula* through the night,
our *thank you* up beyond the swirling stars.

A Paris Bike Anticipates the Day
Our Lady Is Restored

I am a bike in Paris, France, you see?
Two wheels, a seat, and handlebars—that's me.
That Sunday right at dawn I'm taken out
And if a bike could talk you'd hear me shout:
"I'm rolling to the *Île de la Cité*
To meet a lady on this special day!"

I roll along the sleeping boulevards
Past blocks of fine *appartements*. Courtyards,
Posted *privé*, evoke well-tended trees
Beside a fountain for the *bourgeoisie*.
My favorite fountains, *au contraire,* are seen
Where open hydrants flush the gutters clean.

I take a short cut through a graveled park,
Deserted but for one ecstatic lark.
My tires crackle, dusted ashen-hue,
Then further on, upon the avenue,
Leave double-helix tracks of ash to dance
The essence of the line, the gift of France.

I shift to higher gear and humming speed
But suddenly I'm braking, taking heed:
For there she rises, *Notre Dame* repaired;
Her bells are calling all through ringing air;
My metal frame responds in perfect rhyme,
Reverberations felt with every chime.

Off the California Coast

The kelp forests are vast
  and tall as tallest trees
below these ocean waves
  where sea lions seek their meat.
We call them forests but
  they're really something else.

The land is moving fast
  as fingernails grow,
two huge tectonic plates
  sideswiping oh so slow.
This coast slides to the north,
  the rest slides somewhere else.

And so, let's turn at last
  to what we've been made for.
As Maker and what's made
  are two, not one, our souls
like waves must roll to shore,
  returning nowhere else.

All Bright Things

At Chartres, we see the stained-glass windows slump
from centuries of gravity, becoming
thicker glass at the bottom than the top,
like waterfalls of slow and liquid sand.

In Athens, temples, sculpture, palaces
had first been painted bright as Disneyland.
But when the paint was gone, we strangely liked
them bleached and bare like piles of human bone.

And in Jerusalem, Ezekiel wrote,
the glory of the Lord rose like a cloud,
paused at the temple door, then floated up
the hill to look back once before the exile.

So all bright things return to dust and cloud.
The psalmist sang, "Go back, O child of earth."
Yet in that cloud is rain, and in that dust
is Christ arisen, making all things new.

III. Backstories

Boomerang

What I throw out to those I love
   Returns unreached to me, to me.
Bow stubborn knees to God above?
   I do if prayer turns round to me.

Slow whirling in an empty sky,
   Whoosh whooshing almost soundlessly,
Sole focus of my ear and eye,
   It all comes back to me, to me.

Yet selfless love I've read about
   And once or twice I've even known.
A miracle, as it turns out:
   Him swapped out for my blood and bone.

Of grace I have the hope for some
   And harken for that final bang.
O almost-soundless savior come
   And break in two my boomerang.

Picking Berries for Grandfather

He'd sit in his old army surplus jeep,
parked up a rise so he might hear the Cubs
broadcasting on the radio from Chicago
three hundred thirty miles directly south,
as we picked raspberries in the summer sun
of Michigan's Upper Peninsula.

We grandkids had to fill our metal pails
with just the plumpest, reddest berries judged
acceptable—swatting bugs, getting bit—
before allowed to climb back in his jeep
to catch the final innings of the game
if, with some luck, the airwaves reached that day.

My brother Tom once packed his berry pail
with ferns, thin-layering the fruit on top,
and proudly claimed his work was done that day.
It fooled our grandpa; Tom heard all the game
while we two other brothers picked and swatted
down in the berry patch all afternoon.

That evening, Grandpa went to boil the berries
into jam. He noticed the boy's deception
yet didn't say a word. When morning came,
he let his grandkids sit up on his lap
so we could steer the jeep to town in turns—
except when Tom's turn came, he was denied.

We thought that only fair. But then we saw
that Christmas what our grandpa gave to Tom:
a case of jam close-packed in Mason jars,
a summer's worth of berry-picking work,
a sweet reminder that forgiveness reaches
out like raspberries, free upon the bush.

God's Own Language

The Hindi service is at nine o'clock,
the Gujarati is at ten. I pick
the later one so when it's done I'll stick
around when people have the time to talk.

And sure enough, my presence in the church
this summer morning raises smiles and nods
from immigrants from India laying odds
this older, gray-haired stranger's on a search.

They're right. This church is where my grandparents
had worshipped God with somber Nordic joy
in Methodist Evanston, Illinois.
Methodist still, this church's declarants

welcome me here excitedly, insist
I sit up front, and lead me to a pew.
There's something in the angle of the view
and sixty years dissolve like morning mist…

I am a little boy. It's Christmas Eve.
We're in my grandparents' church, here to praise
the child they call Emmanuel. A blaze
of Advent candles beckons me: *believe.*

We sing an opening hymn, we all sit down,
but when the pastor speaks, I start to laugh
because for all the elderly's behalf
tonight's in Swedish—what a funny sound!

My giggles runneth over while, in anguish,
my mother elbows me to hush and heed.
But Grandma has a plan, that clever Swede,
whispering, *Hear that? That is God's own language…*

Now I am back among South Asian saints.
The Gujarati done, it's almost noon.
They say come back—they're adding English soon
in answer to their children's bold complaints.

I promise I'll return. I hope I do.
I thought that all had changed, but what had changed?
Though Swedish, English, Hindi get exchanged,
God's language is whatever makes us new.

The Tongue Is a Deadly Arrow

Penny Knepper, my fifth-grade teacher,
standing at the front of our classroom
told me to be quiet, just be quiet,
stop being the class clown,
and I shot back: Okay, *Penny,*
or maybe: Whatever you say, *Penny.*

I can't recall exactly what I said
but I vividly do recall
that when I used *Penny*
in such a way, with such an expert,
mocking tone of voice at age ten,
she suddenly burst into tears
and left the classroom.

That moment hung in the air,
the blackboard clouding with chalk dust,
my heart beating, the wall clock ticking,
my classmates sitting silent, heads bowed,
none of us knowing what to do,
and I could feel them scared of me,
impressed by me, or hating me
for a power I didn't know I possessed,
and it thrilled and scared me too.

Penny Knepper, forgive me,
wherever you are.
You taught me better than you know.

Iliad in Suburbia

for my father and his friends, born in 1925

My father let me stay up late at night
when his old high school buddies came to town.
They'd sit out in the backyard getting tight
on cold canned beer and watch the sun go down.
There I would sit, a quiet boy ignored,
hoping they'd talk about the world at war.

It didn't happen every time. It's true
that soldiers who had seen the worst stay mum.
But sometimes something in the summer drew
their memories from the dusk, cut through the hum
of mortgages or baseball games they'd seen,
and call them back to when they were nineteen.

One said he wore a Red Cross on his sleeve.
The toughest thing he said he did: Triage.
One met a nurse one warm Pacific eve
who gave him—*what?* I think he said massage.
One served with Patton on his great advance
and singlehandedly drank up all France.

And one, at Anzio with his recon squad,
got trapped behind the German lines. They starved
a week until by chance or maybe God
they found a burnt-out tank. Inside they carved
the ration cans from three burnt men before
they ate their fill, then puked, then ate some more.

Tales like that last one tended to be rare.
Whenever one was told the men grew still.
I'd look from face to face. Each man would stare
down at the ground or in his beer until
a tired joke or subject leveled light
soon brought them back to present day that night.

My dad and all his friends have passed away,
their stories not in books or on the screen.
Achilles, Hector, Stan and Mike and Ray:
The warriors in our midst retreat unseen
to dusty shelves or seldom-opened drawers,
grieving for boys entranced by tales of wars.

Road Hunting

Today his father teaches him to hunt,
driving slow on graveled roads, till some grouse
are spotted drinking puddles up ahead.

His father brakes. The engine's rumble holds
the birds transfixed, heads up. His father gets
out of the pickup truck, takes careful aim,

and shotgun blasts one down to windy death.
You shoot them in the head, he tells the boy.
You'll pick out fewer pellets in your supper.

He says the rulebook states you're not allowed
to hunt this way, but everybody does.
Trying to shoot a ruffed grouse on the wing

in these thick woods would mean you'd hear a whir,
that's all—a whir exploding off the ground—
and watch its blur vanishing through the pines.

Yet age thirteen and full of what is right
the boy declares: *I want to shoot them fair.*
His father thinks and says, *Well, take the dog.*

The boy fights forest choked with undergrowth,
walking an hour, sweating in autumn's chill.
He looks at the dog; she looks at him, doubtful.

They reach a clearing. Suddenly, the dog
freezes on a point. Up ahead he sees
what surely is a grouse, there on a stump.

He slides the safety off. He aims and shoots.
The dog and boy run forward where he sees
he shot a small gray squirrel, not a bird.

He lifts its body, featherweight in hand.
Three droplets of its blood have bubbled, jeweled
upon its gray-furred chest, its eyes gone glass.

The dog is whimpering, waiting for the words
that she's done well—*good dog? good dog? good dog?*—
then cocks her head confusedly because

this human child is trying not to cry
while pulling out the smoking shotgun shell
and heaving it away, far, far away.

Back in the pickup truck—*How did it go?*
The boy, short one shotgun shell, tells a lie:
I flushed a grouse but missed. So you were right.

They drive in silence. The boy thinks how hard
it is to know what's right, how lies are easy,
how life depends on choices he must make.

Hipshot & Tom

Sunday morning, 1965.
I'm ten, Tom's eight.
Comics are in color
in the Sunday *Chicago Tribune*.
Church is starting soon
but Tom says he won't go.
But he will go
because our parents will say so.

Until then, Tom reads
his favorite comic strip: *Rick O'Shay,*
about a sheriff in a Wild West town.
Rick's pal is Hipshot Percussion,
a hard-drinking gunslinger.
Tom's favorite one is when
Rick and his wife are going to church
but Hipshot says he won't go.
Next, we see why.
Hipshot rides his horse alone
up into beautiful mountains
to tell God this: *Much obliged.*

Fifty years later, in Denver,
Tom will die,
alcoholic and living alone.
Next, when I fly there
to collect his few things,
I'll look out my brother's windows
and see mountains,
those beautiful mountains.

Cat and Mouse and Me

My cat, who's kept inside all day, got bored,
somehow slipped into my attached garage,
cornered and caught a little mouse, and gored
that creature's little heart. My quick triage
assigned him good as dead. I pulled off Cat,
put Cat inside, returned to Mouse, then toed
him, twitching still, onto my Welcome Mat,
flicking him in the ditch across the road.

All day, as if in pain, my old cat yowled,
glaring at me with flat, accusing eyes.
"Our bond," he seemed to say, "is badly fouled.
Why did you rob me of my fair-won prize?"
Because our human hearts are warm? Truth told,
we're capable of things so much more cold.

Saint Anthony Falls

We're stuck here, stuck in Minneapolis,
just waiting for our first child to be born,
my wife confined till birth, flat on her back
from a *placenta previa* (it blocks
the cervix and it risks a hemorrhage).
The doctors all agree she cannot move
so in a hospital downtown she stays.

Back home in Chicago, our bosses help:
for her, a short-term disability;
for me, a temporary transfer to
our local offices three blocks away
with promises they'll keep my workload light.
My company gets me a hotel close.

My wife grows bored, especially by the food.
She has me smuggle takeout Vietnamese
wrapped tight inside a plastic bag so nurses
won't catch a whiff and bust me in the hall.
Safe in her patient room, I say "Ta-dah!"
and lift each lid of Styrofoam. Through rising
steam I can see her eyes pool tears of joy
at fragrant rice in mounds like ice-cream scoops,
at chicken pieces flecked with peppered fire,
and shining bok choy greens with garlic chunks.
She eats it all and feels the baby kick.

It's summertime, with twilight well past ten.
Each evening I sit by her side. She senses
my restlessness, perhaps my growing fear.
She says, "I bet it's nice. Go take a walk."

I walk most nights as she lay day by day.
I walk beside the playful fountain where
the water spills off cantilevered blocks
some giant babies dropped on Orchestra Hall.
I walk beside the Mississippi River
where giant babies made a waterfall

and named it for Saint Anthony, the saint
of things gone lost. "Saint Anthony, look around,"
they're singing, "Something's lost and must be found."

I now see giant babies everywhere.
While watching baseball on TV: The Twins!
My rushing brain hears water on all sides.
I dream one night that my wife's water breaks
and I can't hold the Mississippi back.
O God, I'm not prepared for fatherhood!

My wife observes my panic and suggests
I fly home for the weekend: "Check the mail."
(Does she mean check the male?) I fly. Soon after,
while dozing off to *General Hospital*
on her room TV, she feels the labor pains.
Before my plane is back at MSP
our son is born. The name we've chosen: Sam,
from Samuel, the boy who said to God,
"Here I am, Here I am."

                              "There is a problem."
"What? What?" I'd taxied from the airport, rushed
up elevators to Delivery,
and washed and gowned and masked I hold her hand
as she remains in twilight from the drugs.
"Your son—he isn't well." That's all they say.
I go all bloodless, cold with real fear.
I start in asking stupid questions fast:
"Was it because I wasn't here in time?"
"Should she have gone outside to exercise?"
And then, with dread, "Was it the spicy food?"
They shake their heads: No, no, *and no.* They say:
"We think he has a major heart defect.
We didn't see it on the ultrasound."

O God, I'm lost. Please give me words to tell her.
Take me instead, for I will gladly die
to save this baby's broken heart.

                        "What's wrong?"
she says, suddenly awake, seeing my face.
I try explaining; words get stuck inside.
A kindly nurse named Aavya comes to help.

And then, and then, and then… The transport to
The Minneapolis Children's Hospital…
the surgery… recovery… more time.

October comes. We finally can go home,
driving across the Upper Middle West
where autumn colors blaze the land like flames.
Somewhere beyond Eau Claire, on Interstate
Ninety-Four, it gets quiet in the car.
I change the angle of my rear-view mirror
so I can see them both in the back seat.
My wife is gazing at the fields and trees,
her hand in constant soothing touch with him,
a baby bundled in a brand-new car seat,
no giant but a tiny person, ours.
That's when a strange new peace comes into me
and all that I can say is, "Here I am."
She meets my eyes in that reflective glass
and with a steady smile says, "Here we are."

IV. Readings

Cleaning Gravestones

I keep old plastic milk jugs in my car,
wedged in the trunk and filled with fresh clean water,
along with rags, some safe-cleaning solution,
a scraper, and a few soft-bristled brushes.

That's what I use to gently clean the gravestones
of ancestors I find in burial grounds
as I drive state to state to search them out—
thanks to the help of find-a-grave-dot-com.

I go to work with all of my supplies,
dissolving moss and grime, the sap-stained drips
from nearby trees, the clinging blooms of lichen,
scrubbing and rinsing, reviving names, dates,

the curlicues of decorative design,
a sentiment or Bible verse inscribed,
a single name, a husband and a wife,
or sometimes just the family name IN CAPS.

The granite or the limestone or the marble
now gleams in sunshine. Letters carved in stone
look freshly cut and readable again,
as if the long-passed one passed just last week.

Lately, I've asked myself the question: Why?
Why track down our dead, reclaiming their lives?
Is cleaning gravestones just the first of acts
before I make these other voices mine?

Falling

Genesis 3:8–9

It wasn't nice,
No, wasn't nice,
To be called in the Garden by God.
He called us once,
He called us twice.
Was no answer a thing He thought odd?

He must have known,
We were His own,
He presumably knew what we did.
Or was He stunned
By what we'd done?
We refusedly shut up and hid.

That's us inside,
We hide, we hide,
As He's calling our names in the dusk.
And though we all
Regret the Fall,
To be falling is thrilling to us.

The Apostle in the Boat

Matthew 14:22-33

No, Matthew's gospel doesn't mention me
when I was in that boat, wrestling that sail.
But someone had to do it—I could see
the waves were high, the wind a roaring gale.

The others wouldn't help, saying they were shocked,
spotting our reckless rabbi suddenly
walking on water, then our stubborn ox—
yeah, *Peter*—trying to walk like he was He.

(That's *so* Peter: first to speak, first to act,
pushing his pushy self against the master,
as if that made him Number One in fact,
as if he'd get to heaven even faster.)

The sail was flapping wildly but I roped
it to the mast of that old fishing tub,
and I confess a part of me had hoped
his blah blah blah would turn to blub blub blub.

But Peter didn't sink. He cried, *Lord, save me!*
Our rabbi heard his cry and, reaching out,
rescued him, rebuking that big bald baby:
O you of little faith—why did you doubt?

Read that again: little *faith?* Don't you see?
That's *Peter*—who later denied our Lord!
But since then, something changed and burned in me,
in all of us. A different wind has roared.

I felt that wind the day I died for Jesus,
the day they told me, *Step into the storm
if you believe.* I did, knowing He sees us
walking to Him, now in a perfect form.

Waiting in Line for Communion

You stand. You do not shuffle, taking strides
whenever gaps before you open up.

Where do you put your hands? Like actors do
on stage, fingers relaxed, hands at their sides.

You look around. No, don't. Look straight ahead
and concentrate on what it all should mean.

What does it mean? *Remembrance*—that was it.
Re. Member. Reassembled body parts?

Don't joke around, you're nearly to the front.
You want to pray. You almost pray. But then,

you're kneeling on a cushion at the rail,
a small round wafer's pressed into your palm,

and you can feel it searing like a nail
hammered into your hand. Now you remember.

Tyndale

Your words, six hundred years old, fill our minds:
my brother's keeper and *let there be light,*
it came to pass and *seek and ye shall find,*
plain-put so in faith we'll *fight the good fight.*

What's that you said? The boy who drives the plow
should know more of the scriptures than a priest?
They strangled you for that, then turned their scowl
on liberties the printing press increased.

If you were with us now, what would you think?
New ways to twist and warp old words have risen,
and those who will not bow to power and shrink
soon find themselves invisibly imprisoned.

Revival? Is it possible today?
Translate us once again and show the way.

Lincoln According to My Great-Great-Grandfather

I never saw him after the election.
He caught the train from Springfield and was gone.
I glimpsed him working party politics,
That smokehouse of ambition, greed, and lies.
But he was from Illinois. Me? Wisconsin.
Him? Moderate. Me? Abolition Now!

You couldn't miss him—rawboned ugly man
Tall as the trees my Pinery Boys cut down
Each winter in our Northern woods, the motto
For my newspaper blazing from my pages:
The Union Forever! Slavery Never!
He didn't spark such fizzy fireworks. No,

He played a deeper game we couldn't see.
I traveled to Chicago—our convention,
Packed in that barn the papers called The Wigwam,
Built in one month to hold ten thousand men
Who screamed and schemed and strong-armed party men
Like me to nominate him. So we did.

Forgive us, God, we did. That man who tried
To play the moderate saw moderation
Collapse. The South had always itched to fight
And I was sick of waiting for a time
When everyone breathed free, both Black and White.
Named a colonel, I took my boys to war.

This letter must conclude. My regiment
Is camped nearby a lonely church called Shiloh—
Means "Place of Peace." It makes me think of him:
If he will bring on freedom's second birth,
Or fail, or if his infant will be stillborn.
It's dawn—I hear a rising sound of battle.

Longfellow After His Loss

What fortitude the man possessed, his wife
on fire that afternoon, her sudden shriek
waking him from his nap into a nightmare.
He wrapped her with his body, doused the blaze,
   but soon she died and he was left
     severely burned.

Someone in such a grief might tell a friend,
"I still see flames." Not him. Instead, he settled
down to translation: all of the *Commedia*—
Inferno, Purgatorio, Paradiso—
   where Dante meets her, she who died,
     for whom he yearned.

Willa Cather at Age Seventy-Three

She fell asleep more often after lunch,
a thing she never did when she was young
and strong, forever in motion, mind clear.
Today she found herself alone, disturbed.
Where was she? France? Nebraska? Santa Fé?
She wrote so many places into truth.

Edith returned, apologizing quickly
for leaving her—*Just clearing off the plates.*
She nodded, almost falling back to sleep,
and then remembered what she had to say.
Edith was told to handle one last task:
to burn her papers once she died. *You promise?*

Yet Edith wouldn't promise but protested
by pointing to the desk and manuscript.
She looked at it and saw another place,
another time, emerging into form:
her cherished France six centuries ago,
where she preferred to live, not here, not now.

Remind me where we are, she said. *New York,*
was the reply. Oh, yes, but it had changed.
She'd used these crowded cities of her life
to reach the empty spaces she could fill
with bright embodied souls. Finally, she spoke:
I'm sure New York has good incinerators.

Afterwards Edith said, *That's what she told me,*
explaining all the burning when she died—
her drafts, those letters, and her final novel.
She's buried where she wished to be: New Hampshire.
Since Edith died they're side by side again,
their gravestone carved with *Truth and Charity.*

Elvis at Graceland, 1958

His mama died, the woman he adored.
Everyone said they never saw a boy
so devastated—weeping, sobbing, wailing
for days while crying out, *She's all I lived for.*

The boy was twenty-three years old, the king
of rock and roll, a sudden millionaire,
yet still at heart a Mississippi child
who grew up poor, who wanted everything.

He bought his mama and his daddy this—
a Memphis mansion on an oak-groved hill.
Now half a million people come each year
to file past the glamor and the glitz.

Some stand in awe, his greatness verified.
Some smirk at what they see as tackiness.
But then at last we view the bedroom that
his mama used, unchanged from when she died:

Here, simple country dresses, pink and blue,
are seen hung in her closet, just a few,
these simple dresses telling us the tale
much better than the glitz will ever do.

Take an Ear

When some big loudmouth makes a crack,
some *I hate Christians* rant-attack,
I want to beat him to a pulp.
Which isn't Christian. So, I gulp
it down and don't—*but dream I did.*

It's like when Peter sliced that ear
off Malchus as the end drew near
and Jesus said, *No more of this!*
Our Lord accepted Judas' kiss
then touched that ear and healed it.

These days the world seems locked in fear
that words alone may slice an ear.
Yet we know ears are surely healed
by one to whom we choose to yield,
as peaceful Christians need admit.

Famous Graves

Napoleon's *Les Invalides*
    is where they locked him in.
That huge sarcophagus we see
    prevents us swiping him.

Emily Dickinson lies fenced
    within her family plot.
She'd smile at that—its little sense—
    as if she could get out!

The Reverend Martin Luther King
    rests by reflecting pools.
He's Baptist so we know he swims,
    but that would break the rules.

Today these graves are deathly chilled,
    with time they fill with rot.
Except beside Moriah's Hill
    a grave was filled—then not.

That empty tomb is empty still,
    its tolling bell a knock.

The Humor of Christ

John 4:4–26

Lady's yanking up a bucket of water from a well.
Jesus comes by and says,
"Hey, gimme some of that water."
She's thinking: *Go yank your own water, Bub.*
Then he starts in on Husband Number One,
And Husband Number Two,
And Husband Number Three,
And by the time he gets to The Current Resident
She says, "Oh yeah? How do you know?"
He just looks at her with one of those smiles
That's like, *Cuz I do,*
And she says, "Mister,
I'm drinking whatever you're drinking."

Zoom Bible Study

Can everyone hear me?
I am the bread of life.
Can everyone put themselves on mute?
I am the light of the world.
Who's talking in the background?
I am the good shepherd.
What time is it there?
I am the resurrection and the life.
Does somebody have a TV on?
I am the way and the truth and the life.
Can everyone please put themselves on mute?
I am the true vine.
Are you wearing pajamas?
I am the Alpha and the Omega.
You're on mute, we can't hear you.

Seize the Bread!

My doctor said I'm diabetic,
But here's what's even more pathetic:
To lower carbs my doc then said,
"I want you to cut down on bread."

Adieu baguettes in French cafés,
We'll rendezvous in better days.
Auf wiedersehen to pumpernickel
I loved with schnitzel and a pickle.

Ta-ta to English muffins slathered
With orange marmalade—a hazard?
Shalom to challah that I wanna
Send me to deli-baked nirvana.

O breads of life, I'll miss you greatly.
O Youth, who eat bread profligately,
Enjoy! In Latin, *carpe panem!*—
Before a doctor makes you ban 'em.

Walking Trees

Mark 8:22-26

At first, when Jesus made the blind man see,
that man thought people looked like walking trees.
Why *trees?* The Bible commentators bicker
until by insight or perhaps by liquor
they suddenly catch the quirky point of view
of someone to whom everything looks new.

But what of us? Aren't we still partly blind?
When we see all, what promised peace we'll find
as we the trees find a cross took our place
and what we see we now see face to face.

V. Northwoods

Ice Out

All winter this was ice and snow.
  Now April fires our northern lakes,
the sun returns, the south winds blow—
  it's ice-out day; the water wakes.

Our winter lakes were white or gray
  or black as moonless, starless night.
But now a rippling blue display
  has spectrum-spangled us with light.

Hydrology of lakes tell how
  "spring turnover" occurs. That's when
cold water at the top sinks down,
  warm water rises once again.

The human soul is much alike,
  as every spring I often think.
Beside a melted lake I write;
  as warm words rise, the cold thoughts sink.

Proclaiming Psalm 19 from a Lakeside Dock

Sitting at the end of a lakeside dock,
with solid cedar boards below my chair
but ever-flowing water underneath,
I saw a cumulus cloud towering
like a holy city in the summer sky.

I thought of Psalm 19, the one beginning
"The heavens declare the glory of God."
I phoned it up and read it twice, out loud,
offering my voice to the passing breeze
and to a startled flotilla of ducks.

We're gifted in abundance. One is this:
perception of likeness—*this is like that.*
Perhaps that's how we hold in memory
God's promises, once drifting clouds change shape,
and those who shared those promises are gone.

For a Daughter Leaving Home

Over the waters of a Northwoods river,
Where it widens into a shallow bay,
I take you, daughter, to the lily pads.

They grew like this some fifty years ago
When I first paddled out in this canoe.
Before you go, I wanted you to see them

Flowering white on floating disks of green.
No one's allowed to pluck them out, and so
I lift one gently with my paddle blade.

Breathe in its fragrance. See how it depends,
Below a pad striped purple underneath,
Upon a rope-like stem that's rooted down

Within the riverbed, withdrawing for
The winter freeze to rise again each year.
My lecture done, I gently place it back.

The summer soon is gone and then you'll move
Two thousand miles to California's coast.
Rivers of your own lead you to your life.

Prayer As Weather Moves In

Our house is on a quiet lake
facing northwest some fifty miles
southeast of Lake Superior.

Which means our storms throughout the year
can be seen long before arriving,
rising in clouds like mountain ranges.

I sit along our shoreline watching
these storm fronts move and split and change
to every color, every form.

I take a book; it might be hours
until the weather will arrive.
And yet I find I can't read long

because I'd rather read the sky
whose author writes: *Just take your time
and watch. Now talk to me. I'm here.*

Trespassers

It wasn't ours:
The timber king from long ago had owned it
and his descendants deeded it in trust
to stay as everyone had always known it—
     an island wild.

Today it towers
above the lake across from where we all
spent summertime—an island with its thrust
of hill and untouched pines. There I recall
     a trespassed child.

He was our son.
When he was eight, I paddled a canoe
with him out to that island's shore and pulled
it up into the forest out of view.
     Then we explored.

And just for fun,
once we had rambled all around its woods,
we built a hut from logs of pine trees culled
from deadfall, roofed with pine boughs like a hood,
     and pine-bough floored.

We worked all day,
then, pleased, we sat inside our rustic palace,
we drank from our canteens, and ate a snack.
We talked and talked. Of what? All I recall is
     pine-scented air.

He passed away
the winter after that—a heart defect.
Twenty-five years later, I paddled back,
trespassing where we once had built. I checked:
     Young pines grow there.

Past Peak

Not peak I like but just a little past
is best for autumn days I've always found,
when colors fade, leaves fall to gold the ground,
and edge the roads and lanes where they've amassed.
Like how one maple always is the last
to shed its red to bare trees all around,
or how the woods are silent till a sound
strikes as a deer is flushed and bolts off fast.
For at their peak, fall colors prove us fools
by tempting thought that things will never change.
Of course they do, they die. And so it's wise
to live along the downward slope, where rules
are set in time we cannot rearrange.
Like leaves we fall, believing we will rise.

Cold Tonight

It's cold tonight, a record cold, just like
that night when we first kissed. Remember that?
Our faces cold, our lips so warm. Ah, love,
so young, how could we know that time would strike
its hammer blows, and whip away our hat,
our coat, our right-hand then our left-hand glove?

It left us shivering, stripped down to the bone.
We had nowhere to turn but me to you
and you to me. And now that we are old
I feel a very springtime all our own,
I see the flower of your soul anew,
I find at last what can outlast the cold.

Advent

Around December first, the summer people
All have gone. Some had stayed to see the fall
And some for hunting season—all have gone.

We walk deserted roads. The first snows came
But dried away to traces in the ditch
And snowy patches on the forest floor.

In town, the Christmas lights are blinking bright,
The tourists few. The locals seem subdued,
At peace with what some still call Advent time.

It's dark by four. We light a fireplace fire.
We have a drink and share a meal and read
Until it's time to go to early bed.

Outdoors to fetch tomorrow's wood, I stand
Beneath the stars. It's moonless, clear and cold.
The constellations reach like outspread hands.

Star bright but not at all a silent night,
There seems to be a constant trembling—
Someone surely there, someone almost here.

Notes on Some Poems

Beautiful Are the Feet: Inspired by the 2019 production of *Romeo and Juliet* at The Old Globe Theatre, San Diego, California.

Storefront Theater: The setting uses details from several storefront theaters in Chicago, in particular The Gift Theatre and Chicago Dramatists.

Twapandula: For the gracious people in the villages of Bié Province, Angola.

Hipshot & Tom: The daily comic strip *Rick O'Shay* was created by Stan Lynde and distributed in syndication to newspapers around the world from 1958 to 1977.

Saint Anthony Falls: The author thanks the nurses, doctors, and other staff of The Metropolitan Medical Center in Minneapolis (now closed) and The Minneapolis Children's Medical Center (now Children's Minnesota) for the tender care they gave his wife and newborn son.

Lincoln According to My Great-Great-Grandfather: This ancestor of the author is Col. James S. Alban, a Wisconsin politician, editor of the newspaper *The Plover Herald,* and commander of the 18th Wisconsin Volunteer Infantry Regiment. He was killed at the Battle of Shiloh, April 6, 1862.

Willa Cather at Age Seventy-Three: Edith Lewis was Willa Cather's companion for nearly forty years and, after Cather's death in New York City in 1947, wrote the loving and perceptive biography, *Willa Cather Living: A Personal Record.*

The Humor of Christ: In tribute to Elton Trueblood's 1964 book of that title.

Acknowledgments

The author thankfully acknowledges the publications in which these poems first appeared. Some poems are slightly revised for this collection:

Alabama Literary Review: "Elvis at Graceland, 1958," "*Iliad* in Suburbia," "Matisse After the Liberation," "The Tongue Is a Deadly Arrow," "Willa Cather at Age Seventy-Three"

America magazine: "The Sorrows of Migration"

Better Than Starbucks: "For a Daughter Leaving Home"

The Christian Century: "Advent," "Apocalypse Is Beautiful," "The Apostle in the Boat," "Boomerang," "Cat and Mouse and Me," "Church Going Online," "Dutch Windows," Elegy for Eulogies," "Falling," "Fearful Prayer of a High-Rise Developer," "Foreign Studies," "Ghost Light," "God's Own Language," "Hipshot & Tom," "The Humor of Christ," "Prayer as Weather Moves In," "Singapore Men's Bible Study," "Storefront Theater," "Waiting in Line for Communion," "Walking Trees"

Dappled Things: "Beautiful Are the Feet," "Cold Tonight," "The Glorious Order of Things," "Longfellow After His Loss," "Off the California Coast," "A Paris Bike Anticipates the Day Our Lady Is Restored," "Past Peak," "Picking Berries for Grandfather," "Saint Anthony Falls," "Twapandula"

First Things: "All Bright Things"

Light: "Seize the Bread!"

The Lyric: "Ice Out," "Our Neighbor Who Now Waits" (originally titled "Awaiting Your Return")

Modern Age: "At the Comédie-Française," "Lincoln According to My Great-Great-Grandfather"

The North American Anglican: "Take an Ear," "Tyndale"

Poems For Ephesians: "Bowl of Strawberries, Bowl of Milk"

Reformed Journal: "Going Through a Church Split," "Proclaiming Psalm 19 from a Lakeside Dock"

The Windhover: "Famous Graves," "This Week's Deaths by Guns in Chicago," "Zoom Bible Study"

Six poems in this collection ("Advent," "Boomerang," "Falling," "Ghost Light," "Singapore Men's Bible Study," and "Storefront Theatre") were reprinted in the anthology *Taking Root in the Heart: A Collection of 34 Poets from The Christian Century,* edited by Jill Peláez Baumgaertner, Paraclete Press, 2023.

Steven Ward Peterson was born in Chicago and grew up in its suburbs. He had a long career as a business writer for an international consulting firm, posted in Paris, Singapore, and the USA. He left that career to write plays, several of them produced in theatres around the United States: *The Invasion of Skokie, Affluence, The Actuary,* and *Paris Time.* When the Covid pandemic closed the theatre world, he turned to writing poetry appearing in *Alabama Literary Review, The Christian Century, Dappled Things, First Things, Light,* several other magazines, and the anthology *Taking Root in the Heart* (Paraclete Press). He and his wife, Betsy Peterson, the founder of The Children's Heart Foundation, live in Chicago and northern Wisconsin. *Walking Trees and Other Poems* is his first poetry collection.

www.ingramcontent.com/pod-product-compliance
Ingram Content Group UK Ltd.
Pitfield, Milton Keynes, MK11 3LW, UK
UKHW041825090225
454851UK00005B/59